Whit...

WITH...

Shine your Light for Jesus

HARVEST HOUSE PUBLISHERS
EUGENE, OREGON

Published in association with William K. Jensen Literary Agency, 119 Bampton Court, Eugene, Oregon 97404.

Cover design and hand lettering by Emily Weigel / Emily Weigel Design
Interior design by KUHN Design Group
Back cover author photo by Kenna Lynn Photo

For bulk, special sales, or ministry purchases, please call 1-800-547-8979.
Email: Customerservice@hhpbooks.com

Ⓜ is a federally registered trademark of the Hawkins Children's LLC. Harvest House Publishers, Inc., is the exclusive licensee of the trademark.

Shine Your Light for Jesus

Copyright © 2022 by KariAnne Wood, Whitney Wood, and Westleigh Wood
Published by Harvest House Publishers
Eugene, Oregon 97408
www.harvesthousepublishers.com

ISBN 978-0-7369-7410-3 (pbk.)
ISBN 978-0-7369-7411-0 (eBook)

Library of Congress Control Number: 2021943717

Printed in the United States of America

21 22 23 24 25 26 27 28 29 / VP / 10 9 8 7 6 5 4 3 2 1

FOR DAD

The one who is always there to selflessly serve.

The one who will run out in an ice
storm to provide for our family.

The one who is peaceful in loud family dinners.

The one who leads us back to God.

CONTENTS

INTRODUCTION

Hi, new friend!

I'm Westleigh—the older sister. I enjoy journaling, watching romantic comedies, shopping at Target, and having sweet conversations with girls about God.

And I'm Whitney—the younger sister, but only by a minute! I love spending time with my family and friends, dancing in my kitchen, and baking chocolate chip cookies!

Together, we wrote this devotional just for you.

Are you looking to grow in your relationship with God? Do you struggle in your relationships with friends and family?

We want to help!

We love Jesus so much, and he has used these Scriptures to help us in our lives, so we want to encourage you by sharing our heart.

Just remember:

If you are struggling?

If life seems a little hard sometimes?

If you get overwhelmed?

Jesus. Loves. You.

1

SHINE YOUR LIGHT TO YOUR FAMILY

> *God, create a clean heart for me
> and renew a steadfast spirit within me.*
>
> **PSALM 51:10** CSB

WESTLEIGH SAYS…

I love to clean my room.

Is that weird?

What about you?

Do you clean your room right away or wait for your mom to ask you?

It's not that I'm a type A person, but I do like the space around me to be clean so I can get all the things done I want to do. It helps me focus on what's important. A clean room makes me a more productive person.

It's easy to make excuses if my room isn't clean.

For example, if I need to start my homework for the day, but there's a pile of clean clothes sitting on my bed that need to be folded, it can be a distraction. If I don't fold them right away, I can't focus on my homework. So I take five minutes and put everything away. Now there's a clean slate for the rest of my tasks.

Just like the laundry, sometimes we can so easily get overwhelmed by the little or big mountains in front of us. But God tells us there is always a new day to create a fresh slate (and a clean room). It's just like Lamentations 3:22-23 says, "The steadfast love of the Lord never ceases; his mercies never come to an end; they are new every morning; great is your faithfulness" (ESV).

His mercies are new when?

Every morning! So when you've had a bad day and you got in a fight with your brother or sister, you get to try again to be kind and work it out the next day. Or if you've been putting off cleaning up your space? Our God loves us so much, he forgives us. When I'm stressed-out, I like to reflect back on this verse and be reminded that the Lord is so good and can give me a restart so I can look like him more today. So if you've been putting off something you didn't want to do (like cleaning your room)?

Today is a new day.

LORD,

Help me remember that you still love me even when I am a mess. Help me accept every day as a new blessing and a clean start to try to be like you. Lead me to be a better sister and godly daughter today.

AMEN.

> *Do not withhold good from those who deserve it when it's in your power to help them.*
>
> **PROVERBS 3:27**

WHITNEY SAYS…

M y mom is a complimenter.

She's always making other people feel special by noticing nice things about them.

One day we were talking about compliments, and she said something that made me think: "Complimenting others gives me so much joy. Why would I withhold a compliment from someone when it might make them happy?"

She's right.

God shows us in Proverbs that we shouldn't withhold good from others. I believe he wants to encourage us to compliment others.

Could you add compliments to your day? Maybe your sister got a new shirt and you think it is cute. Why not tell her?

Compliments are worth sharing.

Just like our gifts and talents.

God doesn't want us to keep the gifts he has given us to ourselves; he wants us to share them. I believe God also encourages us to use our talents and abilities to serve others.

God has truly blessed me with people in my life who can help me. For example, a friend of mine who is a few years older than me has helped me tremendously with dance. She has worked with me when I struggled and showed me the skills I needed to succeed with my dance tryouts.

She knows so much more about dance than I do, but she didn't withhold her dance ability from me. Instead, she used her gifts to help me grow as a dancer, just like God instructs us to do.

I want to encourage you to do the same for others. It may be through a sporting ability, something you are good at, or simply holding the door for someone.

You and I can use our talents to help our families in some way.

What abilities do you have?

Who can you help today? Who can you encourage today?

DEAR GOD,

Thank you for the good news of Jesus dying on the cross for my sins. Will you help me to keep my eyes open to opportunities to help my family? Thank you for being right there with me wherever I go. Thank you that I don't have to do the things you ask me to alone. Will you give me the strength to help those in my life who need it? Thank you, God. In your awesome name I pray,

AMEN.

> *Listen, my son, to your father's instruction,*
> *and don't reject your mother's teaching,*
> *for they will be a garland of favor on your*
> *head and pendants around your neck.*
>
> **PROVERBS 1:8-9** CSB

WESTLEIGH SAYS…

How do you get along with your parents?

Do you talk to them?

Do you let them know how your life is going?

They want to be there for you.

It's so important to build a relationship of trust and good communication with your parents.

Why?

You are going to need them.

As you get older and become a teenager, there will be many things you will have to navigate with your parents. There's going to be a lot to talk about, like relationships, curfews, drivers ed, friend choices, and so much more.

You are going to have to have difficult conversations with them.

It's not going to be easy sometimes to let them know what you are feeling, but it's so important to keep that communication open.

Here's the thing.

Your parents are so much wiser than you think.

And even though they may tell you no when you really want to hear yes—like when you want to do something they see as questionable—they care.

They care about you *so* much.

All your parents want is for you to be happy and safe. Now as a teenager, there have been several times that my parents have stood firm and told me no. For example, one night I wanted to go to a party with my friends at a girl's house I didn't really know.

I was so excited and ready to go when my parents looked at each other (*you know—with that hesitant, not-that-fun look*) and said they thought I should stay home that night.

At the moment I was sad and didn't completely understand why they were asking me to do something I didn't want to do. But later I realized that it was the right decision, and they kept me safe.

Pay attention to the lessons your dad teaches you and the lectures your mom gives you.

God has them there to equip you and help you follow him.

What can you do to honor your parents today?

DEAR GOD,

Thank you for blessing me with amazing parents. Thank you for reminding me to listen to them. Help me to listen well today and, most importantly, look to you for guidance.

AMEN.

> *Long ago the LORD said to Israel:*
> *"I have loved you, my people, with*
> *an everlasting love. With unfailing*
> *love I have drawn you to myself."*
>
> **JEREMIAH 31:3**

WHITNEY SAYS…

The other day, my mother got upset with me for not cleaning my room.

She reminded me and reminded me and reminded me.

But I got busy and worked on other things I thought were more important.

And my room stayed dirty.

When she walked in and saw my clothes all over the floor and my homework and books in my chair, she was so frustrated.

I felt terrible that I forgot.

I cleaned it up, but I still felt sad and worried she was still mad at me.

And then?

We talked, and she hugged me and told me she loved me.

I'm so happy that my mom loves me even when I forget to clean my room.

That's just like our relationship with God.

Do you believe God loves you?

I mean, not just like a little.

A lot.

Even when we mess up, even when we make poor choices like not cleaning our rooms, God still loves us. (*Our moms do too.*)

I remember in middle school when I started to read my Bible and pray to God. It helped me truly understand how much he loved me.

Do you ever get frustrated when you mess up?

I know I do.

Many people who start to follow Christ hesitate to accept his love because it's hard to believe that a God who is perfect would love people who are sinners like us, but you know it's true!

He sees all of us.

Sometimes when I don't feel loved by others or think people who get to know me better won't like me, I remember that God sees all of me and still loves me.

Wow.

I think when it comes to following God, it's easy to worry when we mess up. I am so happy to have a God who loves me.

Messy room and all.

Have you messed up lately?

God still loves you too.

Hi, GOD.

Thank you for seeing all of me and still loving me. Thank you for wanting to have a relationship with me. Thank you for sending Jesus to die on the cross for my sins so I can be free. In your awesome name I pray,

AMEN.

> *Seek the Lord while he may be found;*
> *call to him while he is near.*
>
> **ISAIAH 55:6** CSB

WESTLEIGH SAYS…

Life can be really hard sometimes.

Even though I have so many blessings in my life.

Even though I have so much to be thankful for.

Even when I have the kindest friends and the best team-mates and the most patient parents.

There are just days when it's hard. I can be having the best day ever, and then a word or thought ruins it all in a second.

And suddenly the day turns into a day full of challenges.

Sometimes I have to remind myself that this world is not our home. We aren't meant to stay here forever. We aren't meant to find our ultimate peace and satisfaction in what today or tomorrow brings.

We don't know what the future holds. We don't even know what God has planned for the next second or minute or day.

So while we are here on earth, God calls us to use our time wisely.

He wants us to be spending time drawing near to him, listening to him, and teaching others about him.

Personally, I hate it when plans don't go my way. I have high expectations of how I think my life should look. I think I have my life planned out, and I want to figure it all out for myself. I don't want to rely on anyone else, and I don't want to ask for help. Then God throws me a curveball and reminds me that it's not about me.

It's hard to call out to God and ask him what to do. We want to be independent and do things our own way. It's hard to hand over the clipboard and pen to him. When we are younger, the future seems so far away. We don't really think about eternity or what life later on will look like, but we need to. We need to wake up every day looking to God and preparing our hearts for the life he wants us to live.

Ask him to change your heart today to serve him.

DEAR GOD,

Remind me that I am not promised tomorrow. Remind me to seek you first and not my own will. You have great plans for my life; I just need to listen and follow. Help me to live like you today.

AMEN.

> *When I look at the night sky and see the work of your fingers—the moon and the stars you set in place—what are mere mortals that you should think about them, human beings that you should care for them?*
>
> **PSALM 8:3-4**

WHITNEY SAYS…

You know what I do when I'm scared?

I look up.

When was the last time you looked at the night sky? Did you see the moon and the stars?

When I was younger, we lived in Kentucky. After living there for years and years, my parents decided it was time to move back to Texas. I was excited, but it was all so much at one time, and I was really scared and overwhelmed. My twin sister and I moved ahead of my parents to Texas while they were getting things wrapped up at our old house, and we stayed with my grandmother.

I love my nana, and I was happy to get to spend time with her.

But sometimes?

I missed my mom and dad so much.

During those first few months in Texas, I spent a lot of time praying. I had some doubts about God. One night I was FaceTiming my mom, and when I told her my doubts, she told me to look out at the night sky.

She said, "Do you see how far away the stars are?"

I looked out at the stars, which were trillions of miles away from me. She said God loved me more than the distance from me to that star.

Me?

The one who keeps messing up and makes mistakes every single day?

It made me feel so happy and secure in God's love.

And now?

Whenever I doubt, whenever I am sad, I just look up at those stars and know God loves me.

And yes, he loves you too!

Do you know that? God loves you no matter who you are or what you've done!

Next time you doubt or get scared?

Just remember the stars.

HI, GOD.

Thank you so much for loving me more than the distance from me to the stars. Thank you for creating me like you did the night sky. Will you help me remember this when I doubt? Thank you for blessing me with another day and I pray for strength to share with my friends and family how much you love them too. In your great name I pray,

AMEN.

> *With the tongue we bless our Lord and Father, and with it we curse people who are made in God's likeness. Blessing and cursing come out of the same mouth. My brothers and sisters, these things should not be this way.*
>
> **JAMES 3:9-10** CSB

WESTLEIGH SAYS…

The other day I got my hair cut.

It was a big change for me. I had long hair, and I got it cut above the shoulders. I couldn't wait to go to school and show it to all my friends.

So many people said nice things that it filled up my heart and made me so happy.

Why?

Words can make me so happy.

I love when my mother tells me my hair looks pretty.

I love when my friends tell me I make them laugh.

I love when my nana lets me know how special I am to her.

When words are helpful, it fills me up.

When words are hurtful, it brings me down.

That's why it's so important to use our words wisely. We must use them to bring glory to God.

We always want to remember to speak kindly to other people, including our brothers and sisters.

Even when we don't want to sometimes.

God wants us to treat others as he would treat them. He wants us to respect and love everyone with kindness and compassion.

And that means everyone.

Even your sibling that you might not always get along with. Your sister who didn't ask to borrow your favorite necklace and then forgot to bring it back.

Were you kind when she finally gave it back?

Or were you rude and hurtful?

Words like that can hurt.

They make you want to say things that aren't nice back to your sister because they hurt your feelings.

You have to remember that your sister was made by God and is loved by him just as much as you are. When you use your words, you should remember that you are representing Christ, and your words reflect who he is.

Ask God to check your heart.

Ask God to give you kind words to use so you can honor him.

DEAR GOD,

Help me to use my love language today to love others like you do. Help me to remember that my words reflect on you, and I shouldn't be using the same mouth that speaks of your goodness to talk bad about your creation.

AMEN.

> *She is clothed with strength and dignity,*
> *and she laughs without fear of the future.*
>
> **PROVERBS 31:25**

WHITNEY SAYS…

Wow. Wouldn't it be amazing to laugh without fear of the future?

Are you a planner?

I am.

I like to have a plan for everything, and I worry if I get off my schedule.

There are people who just live in the moment and take joy in every minute. My mom is like that.

She's one of those people who focus more on the present. When we spend time together, she is so there for every minute of that time.

Does that make sense?

She's not that concerned about what we are going to do later. Instead, she just focuses on the moment and the people she is with at that time.

She doesn't have a fear of the future because she's so busy living in the here and now.

I think that's how God wants us to live.

I don't think planning is a bad thing, but if you tend to overdo it like I do, it can be stressful when things don't happen like you want them to. It's easy to let a messed-up plan ruin your day.

My mom also loves to laugh. She has the best giggle, and it makes other people giggle too. It's so good to just forget about what's bothering you and laugh.

Do you have people in your life who make you laugh a lot?

A few months ago, I was eating lunch at school. My friends and I were talking, and I was about to take a sip of water. Just as I took a drink, one of my friends said something funny, and I spit water everywhere. It made everyone around us laugh so hard.

I think life is so much better when we take a second to laugh. It gives us a moment to breathe and remember that life on earth is too short to get so worked up about things.

Remind yourself to take more moments to laugh and breathe. Take a moment to enjoy the present.

Let go and let God.

HI, GOD.

Thank you for wanting us to laugh. Thank you for creating laughter for us to remember that we are human. Thank you for my mom and that she makes me laugh. You are good, God. Will you help me to trust that you hold the future? In your amazing name I pray,

AMEN.

> *Children, obey your parents in the Lord, because this is right. Honor your father and mother, which is the first commandment with a promise, so that it may go well with you and that you may have a long life in the land.*
>
> **EPHESIANS 6:1-3** CSB

WESTLEIGH SAYS...

I love the movie *Tangled*.

It's about a girl who has lived in a tower her whole life, and one day she decides she wants to leave the tower and find out more about the outside world.

There's a song in the movie called "Mother Knows Best."

It reminds me of what I've heard my entire life—"Listen to your parents; they're older and wiser!"

I get it. I understand, but sometimes I feel like my parents aren't listening to me or what I have to say.

So frustrating, right?

You just want parents to *hear* you, and sometimes you feel like they're not even listening.

My mom and I have our moments, but starting in middle school, we promised ourselves we would never go to bed angry. Anything we have to say or any conflict we want to resolve needs to be worked out that day so we don't carry it over to another day.

I try my best to listen to the wisdom of my parents and what they think is right.

It is *so hard*.

Sometimes I just want to yell at them and fight back.

I want to explain my side of the story and tell them they aren't listening to me.

But just between us? If I sit and think about it, I can't really remember a time when I've fought with my parents about something and then later didn't realize they were right.

My parents have looked to the Lord for guidance as they have raised me, and that's the best thing they could have done.

My parents aren't perfect.

But neither am I.

God is perfect and his ways are best.

If we use him to help us, it makes the teenage years so much better.

What can you listen to your parents about today?

DEAR GOD,

Help me to remember that my parents care so much for me and want me to draw near to you. Help me to be quick to listen to them and not fight back when I don't understand or don't think they're fully getting my point. Lord, you're helping them see what is best even when I cannot see it. In your name,

AMEN.

> *I believe that I shall look upon the goodness of the LORD in the land of the living! Wait for the LORD; be strong, and let your heart take courage; wait for the LORD!*
>
> **PSALM 27:13-14** ESV

WESTLEIGH SAYS…

I feel like I'm always waiting.

Whenever we have a birthday, I always ask my mom, "What do we get to do now?"

I just want to grow up and get to do all the amazing things I see other older kids get to do. It seems like I'm going to have so much more fun when I get older. I just want to click a button and fast-forward to then.

But what if that's not what God wants for us?

Does he really want us to run until we reach tomorrow?

And when we get what we want, to just run toward the next thing?

Have you ever thought about why God has waiting periods? For example, moms have to wait nine months for their babies. Or it takes months of being engaged to prepare for a wedding.

God uses those waiting periods.

He uses the pregnancy time to prepare a mother physically and mentally to bear a child. The time before a wedding is important too. The bride and groom go to counseling and prepare their hearts to unify together as a couple.

Tomorrow is exciting.

It seems like tomorrow is going to be so much better.

We get so caught up in looking forward to tomorrow that we forget about today.

There is so much that God wants us to accomplish today during the waiting period. There are seeds to plant, like maybe God seated you at the Christmas dinner table so you could talk to that one cousin and invite her to church. You might be the only one who reminds her of who she is in Christ and pours into her. Ask God to share who he has called you to share with and all the things he still has for you to do in this season right now.

What is God teaching you right now as you're waiting for middle school or high school?

Are there people in your classes that you know you might not interact with next year?

What is God telling you?

DEAR GOD,

Help me to stop looking so much into what tomorrow holds that I lose sight of the people you want me to interact with and the things you are trying to teach me today. Help me to remember to breathe and look around because life won't look the same tomorrow. Show me how to love like you do. In your name,

AMEN.

2

SHINE YOUR LIGHT TO YOUR FRIENDS

> *There are "friends" who destroy each other,*
> *but a real friend sticks closer than a brother.*
>
> **PROVERBS 18:24**

WHITNEY SAYS…

This morning we talked about friends at church.

Friendships can be hard.

When you read this verse, was there a good friend who came to your mind?

One you can smile and laugh with? One you can share your good news with?

Or was there someone who came to mind that hasn't been a good friend to you?

Maybe you thought of someone who brings you down. Maybe you thought of someone who talks very negatively or is rude to you or others.

If that's the case, I'm sorry.

I've been there.

Sometimes people aren't nice, and sometimes we can feel left out in friendships. I remember spending so much time in elementary school worrying about friends. I put all my energy into who I did (*and didn't*) want to be friends with.

It was hard to make good friend choices. I wanted to hang out with certain people so much, even though sometimes they brought me down and I didn't always feel encouraged by them.

Over time, I learned that friends should make you better.

Not make you feel worse.

Now I know that a good friend is someone who brings you up and celebrates with you. Someone who lifts you up. Someone who makes you feel special.

I prayed for a best friend who truly wanted to serve God and who loved Jesus like I do.

You know what happened?

After some time, God blessed me with two!

These girls love Jesus and truly do celebrate with me. They're not perfect and neither am I, but it's much better to have friends who build you up rather than destroy your heart. I hope you have friends like this.

Do you have friends who support you?

Are you encouraging them?

Is there someone you can reach out to who needs help or someone to build them up?

HI, GOD.

Thank you for always being my friend. Thank you for always loving me even though you see all my mistakes. Will you help me to be kind to others like you are to me? Will you show me who my real friends are, ones who will support me and who I can support as well? Thank you, God, for your blessings. In your awesome name I pray,

AMEN.

> *Do not despise these small beginnings,*
> *for the Lord rejoices to see the work begin.*
>
> **ZECHARIAH 4:10**

WHITNEY SAYS…

Do you have a best friend?

It's one of the most fun things ever.

You want to spend all your time with them. You can't wait until you see them. You call them and text them, and when you are together, you laugh so hard and everything seems funny.

I love my friends, and I love spending time with them.

That's exactly what God wants from us.

He just loves us so much, and he wants to be our best friend.

One of the ways a friendship grows is by spending time with each other. You can spend time with God by putting aside time every day to pray and talk to him and read the Bible.

Do you have a plan for reading the Bible?

If you don't, don't worry. Reading the Bible can be intimidating at first. When you first start reading Scripture, you think you have to read it all through from beginning to end. Some people also think you have to read through an entire book of the Bible at one time.

But here's the thing.

That's not true.

There are no rules for reading the Bible. God doesn't care

if you start at the beginning, the middle, or the end. All God wants is for you to spend time with him and his Word. Do you know that God says, "Come and talk with me" in the Bible? God shows us through this verse (it's Psalm 27:8) that even if it's a "small beginning," God just wants us to be with him. Even reading just a verse a day at first is okay.

God is simply happy when you put aside time to spend time with him!

And just like a best friend, the more time we spend with God and the better we get to know him, the more the friendship will grow.

Do you have a quiet time?

Are you spending time with God?

Make time each day to spend with him and read his Word. He wants to be friends.

DEAR GOD,

Thank you for wanting to spend time with me. Help me to remember that it's okay if I don't read through whole chapters when I spend time with you. Help me to choose to spend more time with you each day. Thank you for wanting to be my friend. In your awesome name I pray,

AMEN.

> *For am I now trying to persuade people,*
> *or God? Or am I striving to please people?*
> *If I were still trying to please people,*
> *I would not be a servant of Christ.*
>
> **GALATIANS 1:10** CSB

WESTLEIGH SAYS…

I am *such* a people pleaser.

I try so hard to win the approval of others.

I want them to include me in party invitations and invite me to sit with them at the lunch table and talk to me and listen to what I have to say.

I want them to want to be my friend.

Sounds selfish, right?

The other day, I wanted so badly for my teacher to see me working hard because I wanted to please her. I made a point of going up and asking about the homework and showing her that I knew the answers. I even raised my hand in class just so she'd call on me. After class was done and she walked over and told me what a good job I was doing, I felt so proud.

I thought, *Yes! I'm so glad she saw all my hard work and thinks I am such a good student.*

The truth?

I was not glorifying Christ.

In fact, that thought didn't even cross my mind.

Instead, I was thinking about and putting the focus on myself.

It's so easy to do. When we take the praise off God and put it on us, we are just glorifying ourselves and not representing Christ to others. It's hard to take the focus off ourselves. We are human, and so many times we just think of what we want and what will make us happy.

We want others to think we are special. We want others to want to include us and to be friends with us. We want to make other people happy so they will like us more. So we focus on our desire for attention and praise from others rather than God.

Instead, we should worry less about what others think of us, put our focus on God, and turn our attention to him.

DEAR GOD,

I thank you for gentle taps and reminders throughout the day that this world is not about me. You didn't send Jesus to die on the cross for our sins so we could glorify ourselves and our actions. Fix my thoughts on celebrating you and your love instead of stealing your glory.

AMEN.

> *Work willingly at whatever you do, as though you were working for the Lord rather than for people.*
>
> **COLOSSIANS 3:23**

WHITNEY SAYS…

So many times we think God is in the big things—like when we have a big problem or a challenge or worry.

But did you know God is in the little things too?

God wants us to honor him in "whatever" we do.

And that means everything we do every day.

He wants to be a part of my homework and when I clean my room, or talk to my friends, or even watch television.

One of the places we can honor God is at school. It's important to work hard for our teachers, but it's important to work hard for God too. We do our assignments and our homework because our teachers tell us to, but God is the one we are ultimately working for.

I even try to find joy in homework.

Homework?

You are probably thinking, *Who likes to do homework?*

I used to dread homework. I would put it off and tell myself I had better things to do. There were so many more things that were much more exciting than working on stuff from school.

I get it.

It's not always exciting to do homework, but our willingness to do something as hard as homework and do it with joy can come from honoring an amazing God who has done so much for us. When we work hard at school, this allows us to bring glory to God!

Being joyful in all that we do also allows us to let our light shine for others.

When you do your assignments and homework and listen to your teacher with joy, others notice your hard work and wonder why you are working so hard at school.

And here's something amazing too.

When you do your homework with joy, sometimes it even gets easier.

I challenge you to join me in striving this week to work hard at school, sports, and other activities so you can honor God.

Yep.

All the activities.

Even homework.

HI, GOD.

Thank you for helping me to learn about honoring you in whatever I do, including school. Thank you for the joy that I get when I do things to honor you. Thank you for the opportunities you give me to honor you. In your name I pray,

AMEN.

> *[I pray] that Christ may dwell in your hearts through faith. I pray that you, being rooted and firmly established in love, may be able to comprehend with all the saints what is the length and width, height and depth of God's love.*
>
> **EPHESIANS 3:17-18** CSB

WESTLEIGH SAYS…

I know you've heard these words before. I know you've probably rolled your eyes when your mom tells you or when you walk down your school hallway plastered with these words in pink paint.

But I'm going to tell you anyway.

You are oh so loved.

Not just a little bit.

But a lot.

You're loved so much that a guy was spit on, had his hands nailed to wood, and endured deep, deep pain so you could live and have the opportunity to know your Father.

He loves you that much.

It's so easy to view ourselves as the world sees us. It's so easy to forget how much we are loved.

When I think of my worth as what the world says about me, I forget just how loved I am. If someone makes a comment about my personality or appearance, it's so easy to get my feelings hurt. I feel small. I feel less than. I think I'm not important or unique.

But when I put my worth in Christ?

I know I am loved. I am reassured and reminded that I am known and pursued.

I know you're probably thinking, *Okay, I get it. Jesus died for me. But he also died for a lot of other people. How am I special?*

He thinks you are special. He created you to be unique. He created you to be one of a kind, and he wants to have a relationship with *you*. He wants *you* to talk to him and tell him of your worries and deepest desires. He wants *you* to step into your unique purpose.

Because guess what?

You're not like the girl or guy beside you.

They're running a different race. They have a different journey. They have their own way of racing.

Don't look over at their finish line.

Focus on yours.

And know that God is cheering you on.

And so am I.

DEAR GOD,

Help me to know I am loved by you. Remind me that I am unique. Remind me that it is okay to be different. Help me to look to you and give my worries to you today.

AMEN.

> *Kind words are like honey—*
> *sweet to the soul and healthy for the body.*
>
> **PROVERBS 16:24**

WHITNEY SAYS...

Friendships can be really challenging.

Did you know that? No one really talks about it, but it's so true.

The challenge today is that friendships are lived out loud on social media. You see who gets invited to what party, and who comments on whose posts, and who is friends with whom online.

And that's what makes it hard. It seems like everyone else is having fun.

It seems like everyone else is making tons of friends.

It seems like everyone else has a group.

And it's *so easy* to feel like you don't fit in.

I get it.

This past year the Lord has stretched me and taught me more about friendship than in any other year. I had to learn some hard lessons.

I learned to cling to the friends who bring me closer to the Lord and to distance myself from the ones who don't help me in my daily walk with God.

And along the way, I discovered some friends I didn't even really know I had. For example, I've known this amazing girl for a few years, but I've never taken the time to stop and really get to know her. I haven't prioritized my friendship with her.

Then one night we had a heart-to-heart after church, and I laughed so hard and had so much fun.

How had it taken me so long to realize how fun she was to be around? How had she been there the entire time, but I'd overlooked her?

I was so sad and so lonely, and she had been there all along. Now? I'm so thankful for her friendship.

She has taught me what it's like to be a true friend. She shows me daily how important it is to go to God first, and she has been there for me through some really rough times.

I have been in awe of how God has used her to teach me some truths I needed to hear. Sometimes a true friend tells you things that aren't always easy to hear, but those things can ultimately lead you closer to Christ.

She speaks kind words that lift me up and encourage me instead of making me feel like I don't fit in. She is a friend who helps me grow as a person and makes me feel special.

How can you be that friend today? How can your kind words lead your friend or classmate in their daily walk?

DEAR GOD,

Help me to be that friend today. Help my words to be helpful, not hurtful. Lead me to use the words you have given me to encourage those around me and to help them grow in their faith.

AMEN.

> *May the words of my mouth and the*
> *meditation of my heart be acceptable to*
> *you, LORD, my rock and my Redeemer.*
>
> **PSALM 19:14** CSB

WESTLEIGH SAYS...

Have you ever been talking to a friend from school and you leave the conversation and regret everything you said? It's like you didn't mean to talk about someone else in a negative way, but once you started, you couldn't stop. That's the thing about gossip. It seems harmless. We tell ourselves that we are just repeating what other people say and not really hurting anyone. It's just talk, after all.

And in the moment?

We don't really think through how it can affect other people. It's so easy to see the problems that other people have instead of looking at my own life. Maybe it's because when I gossip and talk about others, I don't have to try to fix what's wrong with me. I don't have to focus on the choices I'm making that aren't the best. Gossiping can be fun for a little bit, but after a while, it makes me feel negative and ashamed and sad.

And the bad thing? All that negativity can take over my heart.

When I've been talking with someone who speaks negativity instead of positivity into my life, it shows. I get sucked into that downward spiral of all the things of this world. I let the ugly thoughts come in and take up space. And then? I pour it out in my gossip.

Instead of focusing on the faults of others and all that negative gossip? I need to turn my focus on what's truly important.

This verse reminds me that when I spend time sitting with Jesus, I focus on the positives in others instead of the negatives. It allows me to change my heart and see things in a new way. I want the desires of my heart and the words I speak to lead others back to him. I need that constant reminder that he is all I need.

DEAR GOD,

I pray you would allow me to speak life and positive words into the lives of those around me. Help me not to fall into the negative trap of gossiping and complaining. I can't do this on my own. Remind me that every day is a new day and that you are there to hear me call out. Help my meditations to be on things above.

AMEN.

> *Ask, and it will be given to you. Seek, and you will find. Knock, and the door will be opened to you.*
>
> **MATTHEW 7:7** CSB

WHITNEY SAYS…

Do you know you can talk to God about anything?

Yes.

Anything.

Even though he is a big, big God, he wants to hear about all the little things in our lives.

So if we make a sports team and we are excited?

He wants to hear about it.

If we worry about whether people like us, or if we worry we won't be able to make friends?

He wants to listen to us.

If we make a good grade on a test?

God wants us to share it with him.

Why does God want to hear all about our lives and our thoughts and our worries and our dreams? He wants to have a relationship with us.

He doesn't just want us to talk to him when we need something. He wants to hear from us all the time.

Did you know you can come and talk to him if you have questions too? This morning I was having quiet time, and I prayed that God would show me the answer to a question I keep asking him about in my life. So many times, I have questions about the Bible or Scripture or something said in church, and I know God will show me the answer if I just ask.

He's here for all the questions, and he's here for all the big and small prayers too.

All we need is the faith that he hears us and that he listens.

The Bible says in Luke 17:6 that even if we have faith around the size of a mustard seed (which is so tiny), impossible things can happen.

Do you talk to God about the small stuff?

Is there something exciting you have to tell him? Is there a question you need to have answered?

He wants to listen.

He wants to hear all about you.

Hi, GOD.

Thank you for being with me today. Thank you for wanting to hear about all the little details of my life. Thank you for being my friend. Help me to come to you more and talk to you about hard questions I have or struggles. Thank you, God. In your awesome name I pray,

AMEN.

> *Just as you have received Christ Jesus as Lord, continue to walk in him, being rooted and built up in him and established in the faith, just as you were taught, and overflowing with gratitude.*
>
> **COLOSSIANS 2:6-7** CSB

WESTLEIGH SAYS...

If they had an award for being the most dramatic person, they would give me a blue ribbon.

Do you live by what your emotions tell you too?

I am so guilty of this. I'm a very emotional and soulful person.

For example, if I'm in a good mood, I want to do all the things all the time. I want to sing songs and laugh and celebrate. I want to shout to the world how excited I am about iced coffee or my favorite song.

But when I'm "not feeling it"?

I catch myself pushing off my homework, chores, and quiet time because I'm not full of joy. At that moment, I'm a little sad and overwhelmed, and it's hard to do the things I know I should do every day.

The discipline of doing what I know I should do, especially when I don't want to, is so hard.

It's just like that with my spiritual life too.

When we go to church camp and I'm in the middle of the mountain top experience, I'm all excited about growing closer to Jesus. When I'm in that joy-filled environment with other Christians like me, it can be so easy to celebrate and shout out praise for him.

What about when I get home and I'm not surrounded by the excitement of camp? Do I go straight to the Bible and read more about Jesus, or do I scroll through my phone? When my friends don't understand what I'm feeling or aren't as excited about Jesus as I am, do I still want to shout out praise for him?

Ask God to give you the discipline to live for him even on the hard days. Tell him your worries and ask for him to fill your heart with joy so your light can shine brighter even on days when you have to do the hard things.

LORD,

Help me to be disciplined and established in my faith so when my feelings are getting the best of me, I can still do what I know is right. Help me not to give my emotions the power to control my actions. Help me to praise you always.

AMEN.

As God's chosen people, holy and dearly loved, clothe yourselves with compassion, kindness, humility, gentleness and patience.

COLOSSIANS 3:12 NIV

WHITNEY SAYS…

I am not a fashionista.

It's so hard for me to pick out outfits to wear. I stress so much trying to put it all together and making my top match my shoes.

Do you ever worry about what clothes you want to wear? I know I have.

I don't think it's bad to be excited about clothes. In fact, I remember a few times when I had a new outfit on, and I felt amazing walking down the hallway at school. One time I had these high-heel tennis shoes that I loved. I wore them with every outfit I could.

I think God wants us to be excited about clothes, but in a way that pleases him. I believe that representing Christ on the inside is more important than the clothes we wear on the outside. It may feel good to wear that new outfit for a little bit, but what your character is on the inside is so much more important.

Being kind to someone and having patience with others is so much better than wearing a new outfit.

Did you know that as followers of Jesus, we are supposed to act like him? We can do this by applying this verse to our lives.

Maybe a friend was rude to you; you can be kind in response. Maybe someone acts harshly toward you; you can be gentle back to them. Why are we called to do this?

These are the qualities that Jesus had even when they nailed him to the cross. He did not respond harshly to the crowds. Instead, he put others first like the thief on the cross.

I know it's not easy to work on what is inside your heart instead of working on what we are wearing, but we have Jesus to help us.

You know what else? Jesus is even there to help us get back on track when we fail.

How can you clothe yourself with one of these qualities today?

DEAR GOD,

Thank you for your Word. Thank you that it is set up to help guide me in the ways of following you. Thank you that you are walking with me on this journey. Thank you for being there even when I mess up. You are awesome, God. In your name I pray,

AMEN.

> *You are altogether beautiful, my love;*
> *there is no flaw in you.*
>
> **SONG OF SOLOMON 4:7** ESV

WESTLEIGH SAYS…

It's so hard not to compare.

My mom always tells me that comparison is the thief of joy.

I didn't really understand what that meant when I was younger, but now it makes sense.

When I compare myself to others, I lose my joy.

I've been a cheerleader almost my whole life.

Growing up, in the cheerleader locker room, I constantly found myself looking at my hair and then the girl's hair next to me and thinking, *Why can't I look like her?*

I'd see other girls that looked like they had it all together and wanted to be just like them.

Or when I picked out an outfit or brushed my hair or walked to class, that same thought always crept back.

It told me I wasn't as pretty as the next girl.

It's so easy to think you're not as beautiful as girls around you, but let me reassure you.

You are stunning.

You are beautiful.

You are gorgeous.

You don't need to have the cutest clothes or have everyone complimenting you all day to know you are valued and adored.

My mom is one of the most beautiful women I know. You know why? Because she has the biggest heart for others.

She encourages women each and every day to know they're rock stars. She inspires them to reach for their full potential and shows them the steps to get there.

Want to know a secret?

I want to be her when I grow up. She is bright and cheery and passionate about what she does. She looks to the Lord for guidance on what to do and how to lead others.

Does my mom wake up each and every day and think she looks like she just walked off the cover of a magazine? No. Is she super cute and beautiful in her own way? Yes! But most importantly, her personality and love for the Lord shine through her affirmations to others and her actions as she goes about her day.

Instead of comparing yourself to others, remind yourself that God thinks you are special.

Celebrate your beauty.

Celebrate the amazing person that is you.

Choose joy over comparison.

DEAR GOD,

Help me be reminded that what's most important is that I know you created me beautifully and uniquely to have a specific purpose.

AMEN.

3

SHINE YOUR LIGHT TO YOUR NEIGHBORS

> *Let us hold unswervingly to the hope we profess, for he who promised is faithful.*
>
> **HEBREWS 10:23** NIV

WESTLEIGH SAYS…

I became a Christian when I was younger.

It was such an incredible experience, but it also brought some challenges.

Have you ever noticed that when you tell people you are a Christian, everyone watches to see how you live your life?

It can get a little overwhelming. Sometimes I need a reminder of why I choose to live my life like this.

Why do I choose not to curse?

Why do I choose not to hang with certain people?

Why do I set my standards for everything based on what God says in the Bible?

The other day I had a heart-to-heart with the sweet woman who ministers to girls at my church, and through my conversation with her, I realized I had lost my way a little bit. I had lost that sense of urgency for the gospel.

Instead?

I was running myself dry trying to please everyone around me.

I wanted to make my parents happy with good grades.

I wanted to make time for my grandma, and I wanted to show up for my friends and work hard for the teachers in my life.

It just hit me hard in that moment in her office, because

I realized I wasn't doing it with a heart of joy and a desire to see Christ move.

My words might have been right, but my actions didn't match my words. I was talking the talk instead of walking the walk.

Instead of having an intentional heart that pursues Christ first, I was doing it so I could get glory and recognition from those around me.

I took two lessons away from that conversation.

You can never please everyone.

And if we don't give God our worries and actions, it's so hard to walk the walk.

The amazing thing?

God can help us take on the weight of the world if we just let him. He is faithful, and we must remember why we put our hope in him.

Why do you follow Christ?

Have you put your hope in God today?

Remember that there's always going to be people looking up to you as a Christian. Don't let the pressure get to you, and shine your light and show your joy to others so that they can see him in you.

DEAR GOD,

I'm sorry. I haven't been faithful and put my hope in you like I said I would. Help me to be better about giving you the glory and looking to you for guidance before I make decisions. Thank you for being faithful. In your name,

AMEN.

So whether you eat or drink, or whatever you do, do it all for the glory of God.

1 CORINTHIANS 10:31

WHITNEY SAYS…

Do you play a sport, or are you a part of a club or activity? I am on my youth group's praise team. I love singing in youth group and playing guitar at church. I love being part of a group of people who love Jesus as much as I do.

But you know what makes me enjoy it more?

When I sing and put my focus on Christ.

If you are trying to please your coach or your parents with your sport or activity, it can be hard and draining. You worry that you might be letting them down or that you aren't trying hard enough, and it can be a little overwhelming. But if you try to honor God as you participate in your sport or activity, you will work harder and get more out of it. By participating for God, it may also be easier to be mindful of others and how you can encourage them to look to God when they are discouraged!

Just like when I'm singing.

When I sing on stage or off, it's my way to praise him.

Sometimes, focusing on Jesus can also give you courage.

When I was in middle school, I played basketball. I remember being scared to go to practice because I felt like there were so many players who were better than I was.

I just felt small.

I just felt like I wasn't good enough.

So I decided to take the focus off myself and focus on praising God with my sport instead. I wrote Bible verses on sticky notes and put them in my basketball shorts pockets. When I played or dribbled the ball down the court, those verses went with me. They helped me be confident even when I was scared to play. When I thought of playing for God, I had more joy than when I was doing it for others.

Is there a verse you can remember when you are scared? Maybe you could stick it on your bathroom mirrors or your doorframe or memorize this verse from 1 Corinthians so you can remember it when you are afraid.

DEAR GOD,

Thank you for giving me joy when I serve you. Thank you for being with me always, even as I participate in my activities and school. I pray for strength to remember your truth so that when I am afraid, it will help me. Thank you for loving me always. In Jesus's name I pray,

AMEN.

A good person produces good out of the good stored up in his heart. An evil person produces evil out of the evil stored up in his heart, for his mouth speaks from the overflow of the heart.

LUKE 6:45 CSB

WESTLEIGH SAYS…

I like to talk.

Wait. Let me correct that. I *love* to talk.

I like to talk about my classes and school and my family and my twin sister and what I'm feeling.

That is a *lot* of talking.

Did you know that what you fill your thoughts up with will pour out into your actions and words?

I notice that when I fill my thoughts and heart up with things that are of this world, like certain shows on television or social media on my phone, I can get overwhelmed. My brain fills up with those things, and then I'm not speaking life and kindness into others. Instead of speaking kindness, I end up gossiping and complaining and whining.

I notice I'm a little more selfish.

I notice I start to see the negatives in others.

And my talking?

It's not something I'm proud of.

But when I focus on Jesus and put him first, when I'm hanging out with positive people who are speaking life into me and empowering others with positive words, then I am encouraged.

I notice that I'm a little more thankful.

I notice that I see the positives in others.

And my talking?

It fills me with joy.

I want to live a life that is focused on loving God and loving others. It is important to remember that what we fill ourselves up with comes out in our daily lives. When ugly thoughts come into our brains, we should try to combat them with Scripture. I want to memorize more Scripture and be filling myself up with the Word so I can pour that out in my daily conversations. We can be more like Christ when we resist the temptation to gossip and store our hearts up with God's Word.

What are you filling your heart and mind with today?

Make your words and your actions be like Jesus.

DEAR GOD,

Help me to fill up my heart with positive and God-fearing words and thoughts. Help me to meditate on things from above and not from earth. I know it can be hard not to speak words of negativity when all my friends are, so help me to find people who want to be more like you and speak life.

AMEN.

> *In his grace, God has given us different gifts for doing certain things well. So if God has given you the ability to prophesy, speak out with as much faith as God has given you. If your gift is serving others, serve them well. If you are a teacher, teach well. If your gift is to encourage others, be encouraging. If it is giving, give generously. If God has given you leadership ability, take the responsibility seriously. And if you have a gift for showing kindness to others, do it gladly.*
>
> **ROMANS 12:6-8**

WHITNEY SAYS...

Did you know that if you have accepted Jesus Christ into your life, you have spiritual gifts?

I'm not talking about talents like being a great athlete or being able to fix hair.

I'm talking about gifts God has given you—like being encouraging or teaching others.

One gift that I believe God has given me is the gift of encouragement. It gives me so much joy to encourage others, and it comes naturally to me. God has allowed me to use this gift at my church.

I am a co-leader of the greeting time.

I like to greet because I love to talk to people and help out new people who come to our youth group. One time I was able to help a family that came through the doors and didn't know where to go. Another time I met a new friend who had never been to our youth group.

We can ask God to give us strength to use our gifts for his glory. It's amazing what he can do with our lives. Some people may have the gift to encourage like me, or some may have a different gift. This verse does not list out all the gifts God gives people, but I think it is trying to emphasize that we all have different gifts.

Whatever gifts we do have, we are supposed to use them to our full potential. It makes me happy when I am using my gifts.

How can you use your gifts today?

HI, GOD.

Thank you for this day. Thank you for the gifts you have given me to use for your glory. Will you show me where I can use them today? Thank you for being with me as I go. Thank you for loving me so much even though I don't deserve it. In your awesome name I pray,

AMEN.

> He answered, "Love the Lord your God with all your heart and with all your soul and with all your strength and with all your mind"; and, "Love your neighbor as yourself."
>
> **LUKE 10:27** NIV

WESTLEIGH SAYS…

Have you learned about punctuation yet in school? You know, commas and periods and semicolons and question marks?

And of course, my favorite—the exclamation point!

Exclamation points are the best, and they are always there when I need them. For example, when I read a verse like this, sometimes I think one of the words needs tons of extra exclamation points.

Like this word: "All." "All" means everything.

It can be so hard to give God our *all* sometimes. We want to keep some things for ourselves and not share them with God.

We have so many distractions in the world around us that prevent us from focusing on God. Social media, television, friends, family, and after-school activities are all grabbing our attention and pulling us in different directions. Those activities have a time and a place, but when do we have our quiet time? God wants to spend uninterrupted time with us.

Sometimes I try to read the Bible or pray, but my mind is racing and I'm thinking of other things instead of concentrating on him. Instead of focusing on other things, he wants us to focus on him. He wants us to set aside our quiet time just for him and give him *all* of it.

God loves us *so* much.

He wants us to love him with everything we have, and he shows us how to love with his example. Does he halfway love us? No. He fully and wholeheartedly loves *all* of us.

We can show our love for him by focusing *all* our attention on him when we go water the plants or talk to a neighbor or put our phones away during our quiet time. Not going through the motions, but truly and completely spending time with him.

When we give God our all, it will show in our actions. Those around us will start to notice and will hopefully see God in us.

How is your quiet time?

Are you setting aside uninterrupted time and giving God *all* of it?

DEAR GOD,

Help me to give you all my heart today. I am so guilty of just wanting to hurry through time with you so I can check it off my list, but help me to fully give you my heart and my attention so I can learn from you and let your will for my life be done, not mine. In your name,

AMEN.

> Lᴏʀᴅ, *you are my God; I will exalt you*
> *and praise your name, for in perfect*
> *faithfulness you have done wonderful*
> *things, things planned long ago.*
>
> **ISAIAH 25:1** NIV

WHITNEY SAYS…

When I first moved to Texas and I joined my youth group, I was so excited.

There were so many different mission trips and activities and events.

But my favorite?

The youth praise band.

In our youth group, we have students lead worship. There's a lead singer who usually plays guitar and sometimes a pianist and a drummer, and there are backup singers as well.

One Sunday morning, I was listening to the preacher talk. I don't remember exactly what he said, but I remember feeling like God wanted me to sign up for the worship team.

What?

Me?

I couldn't play any instruments except a tiny bit of guitar, and I wasn't really comfortable singing in front of people, so I signed up to be a backup vocalist.

It was fun.

And actually not that intimidating.

There were even weeks where I'm pretty sure my mic wasn't turned up or on at all. I didn't care though because I didn't really want anyone to hear my voice.

Do you know that God already has a sense of humor?

Recently they've asked me to help sing with a friend of mine who is an amazing lead vocalist.

I'm standing at the front of the stage, and now they actually turn my mic on. It makes me smile because I didn't realize when I signed up to sing backup that one day I would be co-leading.

You know what else is funny? God has also used my little bit of guitar playing too, because now I help my cousin lead the sixth graders. It was a bunch of small steps that brought me to where I am today.

God has been with me during this journey. It's so cool to look back and see how he has brought me along.

He truly has marvelous plans.

What is a small step you can take with Jesus by your side today? Is there a friend you can share Jesus with? That small step may impact someone else's life.

Hi, GOD.

Will you help me to be bold today? To take steps that you want me to, whether that's talking to someone new or singing at church? Thank you for being there whether I succeed or fail. Thank you for your marvelous plans. Thank you for walking with me. In your great name I pray,

AMEN.

Preach the word; be ready in season and out of season; reprove, rebuke, and exhort, with complete patience and teaching. For the time is coming when people will not endure sound teaching, but having itching ears they will accumulate for themselves teachers to suit their own passions, and will turn away from listening to the truth and wander off into myths. As for you, always be sober-minded, endure suffering, do the work of an evangelist, fulfill your ministry.

2 TIMOTHY 4:2-5 ESV

WESTLEIGH SAYS...

Woah.

That is a lot.

Verses like this aren't always the easiest to read, but I think they are so important for us as Christians.

If you're a believer, it is so important to remember that at the end of our lives, we're not all going to get to go to heaven.

Maybe you have a neighbor that is the sweetest girl in the world, but if she doesn't follow Jesus, then she won't spend eternity with him. That is so hard to comprehend sometimes.

That's why sharing Christ with others is so important. We must always stand firm and be ready to let others know about him. There is such a sense of urgency in this verse. It reminds us that it's not always easy to be a Christian.

That's why we need to look to him. We need to be bold and share his name *even when it's uncomfortable*.

Yes.

Even when it's hard.

Even when you think you can't.

With some of my friends and neighbors—I just don't want to bring up Jesus. It's awkward, and I'm scared they're going to run away.

But if I truly love the people in my life, I should want them to spend eternity in heaven and not have to endure a horrible eternity in hell.

One time I was so nervous when I started trying to share Jesus with a friend. He shared with me that he recently became a believer and was just waiting for someone to invite him to church. Stuff like that makes me wonder how many people out there are just waiting for someone to invite them to church.

Ask Jesus today for boldness to share and for courage to minister to those around you.

Is there a neighbor you can share your heart with?

DEAR GOD,

I can't do this without you. Help me to work up the courage to invite my friends to church. Help me to share about you with them. In your name,

AMEN.

> *Don't copy the behavior and customs of this world, but let God transform you into a new person by changing the way you think. Then you will learn to know God's will for you, which is good and pleasing and perfect.*
>
> **ROMANS 12:2**

WHITNEY SAYS...

Have you ever experienced being different?

Maybe you forgot it was pajama day and you showed up in normal clothes.

Was it awkward?

Were you embarrassed because you were the only one walking around your school who was different than everyone else? You wanted to fit in and blend in with the crowd, but you stood out for one reason or another.

Most of us experience being different in one way or another in our lifetime. Sometimes it's embarrassing. Sometimes it's challenging. But it's also important to understand that being different isn't necessarily bad.

For example, if you are a Christian, chances are you will face being different.

Do you know why?

Sometimes the things that God shows us are important in the Bible are not the same things that are important to people in this world. God's ways are not the ways of the world, and he challenges us to live differently than the world lives.

Sometimes these differences are small, and people don't even notice. But sometimes? Those differences are big, and it can be hard to be different.

Did you know that even Jesus faced being different?

He told everyone he was God's Son (John 15:8), and no one believed him. There have been times in my life people thought I was different because of what I believe in. Sometimes at school, someone might make a joke making fun of Christianity. It used to bother me more when people talked about it, but as I have fallen more in love with Jesus, I am honored to be seen as different. I hope Jesus will use me as a positive influence so they wonder why I do things that can lead them to think about Jesus.

When I look back at when I was younger, I see how different I am now. I am not the same person I used to be

It's all because of Jesus.

Has anyone ever told you that you were different?

If so, you're not alone. How can you avoid copying the things of this world? How can you shift your perspective today?

Hi, GOD.

Thank you for making me different. Thank you for sending your Son to be different so I can follow his example. Thank you for saving me. I pray that I will share your love with others. In your awesome name I pray,

AMEN.

Speaking the truth in love, let us grow in every way into him who is the head—Christ. From him the whole body, fitted and knit together by every supporting ligament, promotes the growth of the body for building itself up in love by the proper working of each individual part.

EPHESIANS 4:15-16 CSB

WESTLEIGH SAYS…

Did you know it's almost impossible to be good at everything?

We are all good at different things.

Some of us are better at cooking.

Some of us are better at playing sports.

Some of us are really good at being strong, encouraging speakers. God made us all unique and special. There is no one else in the entire world just like us.

And because we are all different? We all have special talents to bring glory to his name. I'm not very good at sports, but I like writing calligraphy, so God lets me use that gift to talk to those around me.

You never know when you'll be asked to use that gift. I just participated in a mission activity at my church where we were serving at a local nonprofit. They needed someone to write labels, and no one else in the group liked to write. I got to write the labels, and I was able to use my calligraphy to honor God.

I love seeing those around me using the gifts God has blessed them with to lead their friends and neighbors to know him.

What are you good at?

Is there a special talent or gift that you have? Let God use that gift of yours to grow and share his love with others.

If you really like singing, ask your youth pastor if you could help lead or sing backup on Sundays and Wednesdays.

Are you shy? Do you just like organizing by yourself? Ask your youth pastor if you could maybe help organize the office. God calls us to unite and grow and fellowship with one another. Allow him to use your gifts to love others today.

What gifts can you share?

DEAR GOD,

Help me to learn what my gifts are. Reveal to me what you have called me to do. And while I don't know what you've got planned for me when I'm an adult, allow me to use the gifts I know I have now to serve you. In your name,

AMEN.

Be kind and compassionate to one another, forgiving each other, just as in Christ God forgave you.

EPHESIANS 4:32 NIV

WHITNEY SAYS…

Do you know how important being kind is?

It's a little thing we can do every day that makes such a difference in the lives of others.

Can you remember a time when someone was kind to you? Maybe they wrote you a kind note or gave you their dessert or saved you a seat on the bus.

How did it make you feel?

Did it make your day a little brighter?

Did it make you feel happy?

One time my friend wrote me a really sweet note. It made me so happy that she took the time to think of me. God wants us to be kind and think of others first, just like my friend did for me.

Here are a few things you can do today to be kind to others.

- Open the door for someone.

- Save a seat for your friend.

- Encourage someone else.

- Tell someone thank you.

- Write an encouraging note for a friend.

- Help someone with their homework.

- Let someone know they are important.
- Clean your sister's or brother's room.
- Pick up the living room for your mom.

And here's the thing—when you are kind to others, something amazing happens. You feel so happy and full of joy. These kind actions can make you feel good even as you are trying to serve others.

It's awesome!

Part of being kind is forgiving others too. Forgiving someone else may be hard, especially when someone has hurt our feelings. I know it's hard for me. Sometimes I want to hold a grudge or stay mad. But when we follow God's direction and extend forgiveness, just like when we're kind, it makes us feel better. Ephesians 4:32 reminds us that God wants us to forgive others just like Jesus did when he died on the cross.

Is there someone in your life you can do something nice for?

Is there someone you need to forgive?

Let's try kindness today.

DEAR GOD,

Thank you for loving us and sending Jesus to die for our sins. Will you show me ways I can encourage someone else today? Will you help me to watch out for these opportunities and be excited because you can work through me? Thank you for being kind to me, God. In Jesus's name I pray,

AMEN.

4

SHINE YOUR LIGHT TO THOSE IN NEED

> *Dear brothers and sisters, when troubles of any kind come your way, consider it an opportunity for great joy. For you know that when your faith is tested, your endurance has a chance to grow.*
>
> **JAMES 1:2-3**

WHITNEY SAYS…

Recently, I had a really hard test.

You know.

The kind of test that makes sense at home, and then the teacher hands you the paper, and suddenly everything you thought you knew…you can't remember.

There are tests in school and tests in life.

And both of them can be hard.

God knows that. He knows that tests aren't easy. So he gives us this encouragement. He shows us that tests help us to grow our faith. Maybe you haven't gone through a big trial in your life, but we face little trials every day.

Maybe you got a bad grade on a test and it made you sad. You can recognize that this is an opportunity to study hard to prepare yourself for the next test! Maybe your friend was rude to you and you got mad. You can see this as an opportunity to reflect Jesus through being kind to her.

One difficult situation that truly tested me was when I had eye surgery. One day, I gradually started to lose my eyesight.

The doctor told us that I had to have emergency eye surgery. It was a scary time for me, but you know what?

God was with me. Through this test, I learned more about God's love for me. I'm grateful I went through that experience because now I understand more what people are going through when they have surgery. Facing hard times is not easy and not fun.

But just between us? Tests like that can help us to learn more. Tests can make us better.

Tests can make us stronger, especially if we recognize that Jesus is with us when we face them.

Tests can also help us learn more so we can relate to others who face trials. After having eye surgery, I know a little more about what it's like to have surgery and how it can be scary. Now I can help comfort those who are about to have surgeries because I understand that it is a hard situation.

Will you join me in trying to view hard situations differently?

What trials are you facing that you can see as an opportunity to grow your faith?

Is there someone you can help who is facing a hard situation today?

DEAR GOD,

Thank you for giving me the Bible so I can see my situations differently. Thank you for giving me opportunities every day to grow my faith. Thank you for giving me choices. Will you be with me as I face my trials? In your name I pray,

AMEN.

If anyone purifies himself from anything dishonorable, he will be a special instrument, set apart, useful to the Master, prepared for every good work.

2 TIMOTHY 2:21 CSB

WESTLEIGH SAYS…

What do you think when you read this verse?

Does it make you feel convicted?

Do you ever feel unworthy to be a special instrument to the Lord?

Do you feel like you haven't made the best choices?

I get it.

I understand.

It's so easy to tell yourself, *Oh well, I lied to my friend Sarah last week about hanging out with that friend Julie she doesn't like. God doesn't want me to talk to that girl about him. I'm too messed up and far gone. I shouldn't even try.*

No!

Those words just aren't true! My friend, he *loves* you so much! Every broken, messed up, dirty part of you. He loved you before you were born, and he loves you now. He wants to be a part of your life and surround you with love. He wants you to show your brokenness to the world so others can see his goodness in your life and how he has rescued you.

One of my favorite women in the Bible is Hannah. First Samuel 1:15 says, "'No, my lord,' Hannah replied. 'I am a woman with a broken heart. I haven't had any wine or beer; I've been pouring out my heart before the LORD'" (CSB).

The way that Hannah prayed is *so* inspiring to me. She poured out her heart to Jesus and focused on him with everything that she had.

Was she perfect?

Not even close.

But she loved the Lord. God used Hannah and her prayers and brokenness to bring him glory. He heard her prayers and answered them. He saw her heart and called her to so much more.

Then when Hannah followed God's plan for her life, he was glorified. When we lean into what God is calling us to do and take our worldly desires out of the equation, God can use us to bring glory to his name. We can help take care of those in our community who might need a little extra love by taking them some food or blankets. So many times, we make the mistake of trying to bring glory to our own names or look to others like we have it all together.

But the truth is that it's not about us, it's about him.

Ask God to remind you of this today.

GOD,

Remind me why I am chosen. Remind me that I am not on this earth to bring glory to my name but to yours and yours alone. Help me not to be like Hannah but like Christ. Use me to do your will.

AMEN.

> *Do not throw away this confident trust in the Lord. Remember the great reward it brings you!*
>
> **HEBREWS 10:35**

WHITNEY SAYS…

I f there's one thing I wish I could change about myself?

I wish I didn't worry.

There are days when I don't worry, but there are so many days when I struggle.

I know I shouldn't.

But I can't help it.

Sometimes we look at others and they look so happy.

We think we are the only ones who worry.

If you've ever thought this, let me encourage you.

Worry is something we all struggle with. Honestly, it's something that everyone deals with at one time or another.

One thing that has really helped me let go of my worry is to focus on God. God calls us to have confidence in him. He wants us to have certainty that he is with us and confidence that he is working everything out for our good.

These are the promises God has made to us. When I hear these words, my heart is so much lighter. This is how I know to trust God when I can't see him or feel him.

There have been so many times when he's helped me with my nervousness.

As a part of my high school's drill team, sometimes I get nervous before going out on the football field to perform. God reminded me of Hebrews 10:35 one Friday night right before I went to perform. This verse helped me remember that I have confidence in God. That week with the dance team when I performed—I danced with joy.

When we remember that God can give us confidence, we can do things even if we're nervous because he is always with us.

And the reward when we overcome our nervousness? It's the joy we have in walking in confidence with God. I had joy that Friday because I knew God was with me and that even if I made a mistake, everything was going to be okay.

What are you nervous about?

Next time you worry, instead of leaning into it, ask God to give you confidence in all things.

As you gain confidence, you can begin to help others gain confidence too.

DEAR GOD,

Thank you that I can have confidence in you in whatever I'm doing. Help me to remember you are with me next time I'm nervous. Thank you for being with me always. Help me to share this with my friends. In Jesus's name I pray,

AMEN.

> *I have told you these things, so that in me you may have peace. In this world you will have trouble. But take heart! I have overcome the world.*
>
> **JOHN 16:33** NIV

WESTLEIGH SAYS…

Have you ever had an event in your life you felt unprepared for? Something you didn't have any control over. Something that made you feel helpless.

Like a move to a new city or changes with your family or a snowstorm where the power and the internet go out.

So many events like that happened in 2020. One day the world flipped upside down when COVID-19 showed up.

I remember listening to my parents talk about it and hearing about it on the news. It seemed like something that was happening far away. I had no clue when I first heard about it that it would be such a huge pandemic. I had no idea of everything that was about to change in my world.

And then there were *so many* things and events that changed in my world. It was so scary.

When all we know is shaken, we don't know what to grab on to. Some people hold on to family, but they couldn't be around relatives because of the virus. Some people hold on to staying busy, but they didn't have a social calendar, events, sports, or other things because all that was taken away. Some people hold on to technology, but it wasn't always working or available.

That time in quarantine taught me that the *only* thing I can grab on to is Jesus. When everything else was failing around me. When everything I knew and counted on was lost. When the world changed every single day.

Jesus was there.

It was such a reminder for me. Sometimes I get so caught up in my own little world that I forget to put him at the front of my day.

With the pandemic, my world was rocked, but something good came out of it.

I had a great reminder of what's truly important.

I was reminded that we all need to lean on each other.

I loved being able to see so many people helping each other through some of the hardest times.

God was and is still there for us. All we need to do is reach out to him.

What are you relying on Jesus for today?

DEAR GOD,

Help me to remember to reach out to you today. God, I am so bad at remembering that all these things I worry about aren't promised tomorrow. Help me to set my priorities straight and stay faithful to you.

AMEN.

> *Summing it all up, friends, I'd say you'll do best by filling your minds and meditating on things true, noble, reputable, authentic, compelling, gracious—the best, not the worst; the beautiful, not the ugly; things to praise, not things to curse. Put into practice what you learned from me, what you heard and saw and realized. Do that, and God, who makes everything work together, will work you into his most excellent harmonies.*
>
> **PHILIPPIANS 4:8-9** MSG

WHITNEY SAYS…

D o you ever struggle with negative thoughts?

Oh, good. *Me too.*

I struggle with thinking negatively sometimes. (*Okay, a lot more times than I want to admit.*) For example, during the COVID-19 pandemic when we were all quarantined, it was easy to get sad and nervous.

There were so many places we couldn't go and events we had planned for that we couldn't attend. I was a little overwhelmed and lonely and frustrated, so of course, I started to think about the worst and got scared and nervous. But instead of focusing on the negative when faced with a challenge, God asks us to think about the best.

He wants us to focus on what we can do—to focus on the positive—instead of the negative things in our life.

Here's an example of turning negatives into positives:

I couldn't go to restaurants, but I could stay home and eat with my family.

I couldn't babysit, but I could help my mom clean around the house.

I couldn't go to the movies, but I could watch a movie at home.

I couldn't visit my friends, but I could talk to them on the phone.

I couldn't go to church, but I could watch it online.

Just like God tells me to, I was thinking about "the best, not the worst."

Changing our thoughts from negative to positive ultimately makes us happier and honors God!

What are some negative things you've been thinking about? How can you change those to think on the bright side of things?

Hi, GOD.

Thank you for asking me to do things that may seem hard but will ultimately be for my good. Thank you for blessing me with the Bible, which can guide me. Will you help me to change my thoughts to think about the best in situations? Thank you, God. In your name I pray,

AMEN.

> *I consider that our present sufferings*
> *are not worth comparing with the*
> *glory that will be revealed in us.*
>
> **ROMANS 8:18** NIV

WESTLEIGH SAYS…

Do you ever wonder why God allows bad things to happen?

Why does God bless us with so much but let homeless people go without food to eat?

Sometimes when I listen to the news, it makes me so sad. I hear about something that happened in the world and I want to cry.

It stresses me out.

I get so overwhelmed.

It just doesn't make sense to me at all. Why is our world so broken? Why do we have sad things happen, like natural disasters and family members passing away and sicknesses that affect people we love?

God doesn't want to see us hurt.

He doesn't want to see us in our sadness and worry. He doesn't want us to be overwhelmed.

He wants us to be safe in his arms.

When God created the world, it was perfect. But then, just as he shows us in Genesis, humans made this world broken. We have brought sin in and allowed it to get in the way of our relationship with God.

That's why he sent Jesus.

Jesus came and died on the cross for our sins so we could live in heaven one day. Jesus loves us *so much* that he came here to save us from our sins.

He wants us to love on those around us just like he does.

And that's the amazing message God wants us to hear.

Life on earth is short, but our eternity with God is forever.

Heaven will be glorious. We'll be able to see Jesus and dance. We can't fully understand it now, and we can't understand why bad things happen.

But we do know that we have an amazing God, and when we're faced with overwhelming things, we have to trust him. We have to love and serve his people even when it's hard.

He created this world and us and everything in it.

He wants what is best for us.

He has a plan for our lives, and he loves us so much.

How can you serve him and bless someone around you today?

DEAR GOD,

Help me to remember that while you see my struggles and you are there to help me through them, my pain on earth is bearable, for one day I will get to be with you forever. God, help me to use this time on earth to be fruitful and go tell others of your love. Help me to be selfless today and love like you.

AMEN.

> *Faith shows the reality of what we hope for; it is the evidence of things we cannot see.*
>
> **HEBREWS 11:1**

WHITNEY SAYS…

Have you ever gone on a mission trip? I've been on several with my church, and sometimes the most unexpected things happen.

We recently went on a mission trip to Hungary.

This trip was with my youth group, and on the trip, instead of staying at a hotel, we stayed in host homes. Host homes are provided by people from the local churches we are working with who invite students from the mission trip to stay in their homes.

Every time I go to a different country, it's always scary at first being in a new environment and a new home.

But then?

It always ends up being fun.

My friend and I were lucky enough to get to stay in a host home together with an amazing couple who were both blind. They had the most incredible faith in God, and they loved Jesus so much. We learned a lot from them during our stay. Every day, when we were finished working at the church, the man would tell us stories about his family and the challenges they had faced. He explained that he and his wife wanted to have children, but they were worried that their child might be blind, and so they prayed for their unborn child for five years.

God heard their prayers.

Even though the chances were very slim, they had a child who was born with sight.

Their faith inspired me.

They had prayed faithfully for five years—wow!

It was such an example for me. I want to have faith like that. I want to pray with purpose. Do you need to pray for something in your life? Sometimes we worry about praying because we think God won't hear us.

Just like with the family from our host home, he hears every prayer, and he listens faithfully.

Do you have something you want to pray for?

God is ready to listen.

Hi, GOD.

Thank you for being in control of my life. Thank you that you are with me always. Please help me to trust in you, even if plans don't happen the way I want them to. I want to choose to have more faith in my life rather than be worried about the situations I face. In your awesome name I pray,

AMEN.

> *We know that in all things God works for the good of those who love him, who have been called according to his purpose.*
>
> **ROMANS 8:28** NIV

WESTLEIGH SAYS...

The other day I failed a test.

The teacher handed me a paper, and there was a 57 at the top of the page circled in bright red. I almost started crying.

I should have studied harder.

I should have prepared more.

I should have taken better notes.

And on and on and on.

It felt like I let everyone down, including my family and my teacher.

Have you ever had a day like that? One where you feel like you failed and the weight of the day or year is all upon your shoulders?

Just know that you are in God's hands. You have a purpose. *You are seen.* You are loved. You are valued.

I grew up in a small town where it wasn't "uncool" to pray before lunch or share the gospel. When I started high school, my family moved to a large city with a big and very religiously diverse school. At my new high school, I tried to share my faith with a girl I was friends with. In the middle of our conversation, two other people joined in, and all three individuals were denying my words.

I was flustered and didn't know what to do or say. I felt unqualified, and I was shocked that they were so critical.

I felt like I failed the test.

But the Lord showed me that I needed to learn to hold tighter to my relationship with him. I didn't understand it at that moment, but later God revealed to me from that season of tough conversations with nonbelievers that he was molding and growing me to be stronger in my faith. God has a unique life plan for you and for me. He wants us to seek his will for our lives. I love how the Lord uses circumstances and situations to reveal himself to us. He uses people as well through different conversations and actions. He has an awesome plan for you if you just read his Word and seek his will.

Ask him to share steps of how you can walk into that calling!

DEAR GOD,

Help me to remember these words. Help me to step into the calling that you have for me. Not my friend's but my unique calling that you have designed purposefully for me. You are good, and I will put my trust in you today.

AMEN.

> *What we suffer now is nothing compared to the glory he will reveal to us later.*
>
> **ROMANS 8:18**

WHITNEY SAYS…

This past week, there was a big snowstorm where I live. It was freezing outside, and the roads weren't drivable at all. Many people couldn't go anywhere because of the snow, and they lost heat and power and even water. In the middle of all that snow, it was hard to believe it would ever end.

I knew eventually it would melt and people would get their power back on, but that was hard to imagine when there were seven inches of snow on the ground.

Now here I am a week later, and the temperature is back to normal, and the snow is melted.

It almost seems like it never even happened.

We all have times in our lives when we just can't see ourselves getting past a certain point or struggle.

It's just like when I had eye surgery.

It was right after I started my relationship with Jesus. I spent a lot of time learning about him and sharing him. I was on the basketball team, and it was fun because I could play for God.

Then I started having problems with my eyesight.

In the middle of one of my games, I looked at the scoreboard, and everything looked like mush.

My mom took me to the doctor, and they told me I had to have emergency eye surgery.

It was not an easy time for me. I couldn't read, and I was at home a lot.

But you know what?

God never left me.

I ended up having multiple eye surgeries, and I couldn't see the future because of the storm around me.

But God healed me. Praise the Lord!

I can't play basketball now because of the surgery, but God knew what was going to happen, and he brought dance into my life instead.

He brought me through the storm.

He placed friends in my life who helped me through that hard time. I want to trust that he is in control and focus on helping someone else.

Even when we can't always see what's going on, his ways are best.

Is there a problem in your life you need help with?

Is there someone in your life who could use some help?

Put your trust in God.

Hi, God.

Thank you for the times in my life when you have been with me and brought me through. Will you continue to be with me as I go? Thank you for loving me and never failing me. In your amazing name I pray,

AMEN.

> *You, Lord, are kind and ready*
> *to forgive, abounding in faithful*
> *love to all who call on you.*
>
> **PSALM 86:5** CSB

WESTLEIGH SAYS…

D o you wonder if people would still like you if they knew the real you?

You know.

The parts that aren't pretty that you never want people to know about.

The yucky thoughts you might think sometimes.

The struggles you have.

Sometimes all that ickiness is stuff you can't even share with your closest friend.

I sometimes feel this way.

We are all sinners—every single one of us. We forget people or important things we need to do. We say mean things and don't honor our father and mother. We aren't kind, and we mess up God's beautiful plans. *But guess what?*

What if I told you that someone *does* know your deepest secrets and *still* loves you?

Like, not just a little bit?

A whole, whole lot.

And can I be honest? This morning I woke up and was feeling a little down because I felt distant from God. I felt like he was far away from me. I felt like he wasn't listening.

I cracked open my Bible, and this verse from Psalms leaped off the page at me. I had to find a pen and scribble it down on a piece of paper because I loved it so much.

Sometimes that kind of love can seem unreal.

It's hard for us to understand.

It can be overwhelming to consider how much God loves us and is always ready to forgive us—even when we know we don't deserve it. I want to remember how faithful the Lord is.

He calls on us to do the same and be faithful to him with our prayers and our Bible readings.

If you haven't been spending time with God, he's waiting for you. He wants to help you in the little things and remind you how much you are loved so you can share that love with those around you.

Have you shared your heart and your secrets with God?

He's waiting to spend time with you.

DEAR GOD,

I am so sinful. Thank you for forgiving me of not just the surface-level sins but the deep ones. Help me remember that if you can forgive me and all my sins, I can forgive the girl beside me. Lord, you are so loving. Help me to write this verse on my heart today and look to you.

AMEN.

5

SHINE YOUR LIGHT TO THE WORLD

You made all the delicate, inner parts of my body and knit me together in my mother's womb. Thank you for making me so wonderfully complex! Your workmanship is marvelous—how well I know it.

PSALM 139:13-14

WHITNEY SAYS…

If you look at social media, does it ever overwhelm you?

There are so many perfect people with beautiful clothes and amazing hair. If I spend too much time online, I can get down. I compare myself to others, and I come up short. I feel small. I feel less than.

If you struggle with comparison like me, I want to give you encouragement today.

God. Made. You.

You with the curly hair.

You with the straight hair.

You with the giant smile.

You with the sparkle in your eyes.

You.

The amazing thing is that he made every person unique. God is the one who chose how much hair we have on our heads and how tall we are and what our personalities are like. Sometimes it's so easy to look at other people and compare ourselves. When we compare, we think we aren't beautiful, and it steals our joy. We think we are not enough.

However, this is not true.

God's "workmanship is marvelous"! Just like a beautiful sweater, he knit us together in our mothers' wombs. When I was born, I only weighed two pounds, two ounces because I was born almost three months early. Most babies weigh a lot more than that when they are born. Even though I was a lot smaller, God protected me and called me beautiful even as I was formed in my mom's womb.

He calls you beautiful too. He made every feature you have, whether it be freckles on your face or a birthmark. He loves you just the way you are. He made you special and wonderful and unique.

Remember, in this whole wide world, there is only one you.

You know the girl next to you that you may think has a cuter outfit on or has better-looking hair?

She may be thinking the same thing you are. Be kind to others because they may feel insecure like you do sometimes.

What is your favorite thing about yourself?

Make God happy and celebrate it today.

Hi, GOD.

Thank you, God, for making each of us beautiful in our own way. Thank you that we have the Bible to remind us. Will you help me to believe this and share with my friends that you have made them wonderfully too? In your awesome name I pray,

AMEN.

> *Without wise leadership, a nation falls;*
> *there is safety in having many advisors.*
>
> **PROVERBS 11:14**

WESTLEIGH SAYS…

I wish life had an instruction book.

The book would have chapters on what to do in different situations and tell me what to do when I struggle with friendships.

Or school.

Or church.

Or life in general.

In sad news, life doesn't come with instructions, but I think God has given us something even better.

Wise older women to pour into us and give us wise counsel.

Walking through new friendships, navigating new classes, and dealing with all those new hormones can be a lot. How do you know how to talk to other teenagers, how to balance church and school and family, or what to do when your friend isn't there for you anymore?

Wise leadership!

Once I was having some friend troubles, and I was upset and sad because a friend was being rude and hurting my feelings. I didn't know what to do, and I wanted to cry. I went and poured my heart out to the woman who ministers to girls at my church. She listened to my story, encouraged me, reminded me who I was in Christ, and told me I didn't need to be surrounding myself with people who only pour negativity into me. Now, she didn't say I shouldn't still be kind and friendly to those around me. She just said I should spend more time with those who pour positivity into me.

Wise advice!

I could not have gotten through my teenage years without older women pouring into me and constantly affirming me in what I'm doing in my life. Encouraging me to shine the light that is Jesus within me. I have been blessed to have incredible older women who have helped me draw closer to the Lord and helped check me in the areas of my life where I'm not putting God first.

God still continues to put those older women into my life so I am reminded to live a life according to God's will and not the world. It's so important to seek Christian adults and older mentors who can give you advice and help you through all the tough seasons in life.

Do you have wise women in your life?

Let them know how special they are.

DEAR GOD,

Help me find adult women who will pour into me and help lead me closer to you. Lord, I can't go through life on my own. Help me remember that the advice of those who have already been through what I have is important to help me grow.

AMEN.

> *The LORD your God is living among you. He is a mighty savior. He will take delight in you with gladness. With his love, he will calm all your fears. He will rejoice over you with joyful songs.*
>
> **ZEPHANIAH 3:17**

WHITNEY SAYS…

Is there something you delight in?

Maybe you delight in your sport or club or favorite activity. Maybe you delight in crossing the finish line after running around the track a few times. Maybe you enjoy watching a movie inside on the couch on a rainy day with a fuzzy blanket.

You know what I delight in?

I love making and eating chocolate chip cookies. Warm, freshly baked cookies right out of the oven. They go perfectly with a cold glass of milk. You may be thinking, *I love cookies too, but what does that have to do with God?*

One really cool thing about God is that he will delight in us. Even though we aren't perfect, he cares about us!

Isn't it awesome?

What a great thing to think about as you walk down the hallway at school or the aisle at the grocery store.

God wants to delight in you.

He loves you and wants to have a relationship with you!

This verse also talks about his love. Sometimes it's hard for us to understand, but I think God wants us to think about his love so we don't have to be afraid. If we think about his great love, it can motivate us to do the things he asks us to.

There have been so many times when I feel God tugging on my heart and encouraging me to do things like sit with someone who is sitting all alone at lunch.

If I'm being honest? Sometimes I'm scared. God doesn't want me to be afraid.

Why?

Because I believe that God is with me in whatever I do.

And he gives me the strength to do the hard things.

He wants me to share that he cares about that person too, and he wants them to know about his love for them!

What is he encouraging you to do today?

HEY, GOD.

Thank you for being with me wherever I go. Thank you for not wanting me to be afraid. Will you help me to do the things that you ask me to do? Will you help me to do them with excitement because of your love for me and others? Thank you for your truth today and for delighting in me with gladness. In Jesus's amazing name I pray,

AMEN.

> *In the same way, let your light shine before men, that they may see your good deeds and glorify your Father in heaven.*
>
> **MATTHEW 5:16** BSB

WESTLEIGH SAYS…

Did you know that people are looking up to you? You may not even be aware of the impact you are having on other people's lives.

Right. This. Very. Minute.

Recently I was reminded of this through a discussion with a young girl at my church. I was talking about a situation in my life and how I was dealing with it. Midconversation, I noticed how intently she was listening and taking in every word. She was watching and listening to see how I responded to a very challenging situation.

Wow! How the Lord used that girl to shake me. God nudged my heart with the realization that younger girls are looking up to me. Having others look to you for guidance can seem a little intimidating, and sometimes it can be so hard to look like Christ when we're surrounded by people who don't desire the same relationship.

But we should let our light shine through us for Jesus.

This verse from Matthew is one of my favorites because it reminds me that as Christians, while we may have faith by grace instead of works, we are still called to be the hands and feet of Jesus. We should show him and his love in all that we do by choosing to do good and be a positive light to others around us.

We aren't perfect.

Not even close.

But here's the thing: We don't have to be. God loves us right where we are, and he uses our imperfectness to reach others. It's so sweet to know we don't have to earn the Lord's approval. Instead, we can worship him and ask for forgiveness when we mess up. It's important to remember that nonbelievers and younger generations are watching our actions and words, and we should be a godly example of what it looks like to be like Christ.

How can you show Christ through your actions today?

What are you doing to be an example to those around you?

DEAR GOD,

Let the light of Jesus shine through me. Help my words not to be from me but from you. Help others when they look at me to see you and your love. You are who should be glorified, not me. Help me remember this today.

AMEN.

> *Give thanks to the LORD, for he is good;*
> *his love endures forever.*
>
> **1 CHRONICLES 16:34** NIV

WHITNEY SAYS…

Have you ever gotten a present and forgotten to say thank you?

Even though I know it's important, so many times I forget to say those two little words.

To help me adopt an attitude of gratitude, I look at saying thank you as a way of remembering all the good things God has done. It's also a reminder that he will continue to do great things in my life and the lives of others.

One idea that has helped me to be more grateful is my thankful jar. In my room, I have a jar that a family friend gave me with slips of paper. Each one of those pieces of paper is blank.

When something good happens in my life, I write it down on one of the pieces of paper and add it to the jar. I've written down the names of friends, times when God has used me, and different things that God teaches me every day. At night, I can read one truth from the jar before I go to bed and smile because God is good.

It's a great way to remind myself of all the things I have to be thankful for. The more pieces of paper I add to the jar, the more visible things in my life I can be grateful for. I can see an entire jar full of thankfulness. Thankfulness for the cool things that God has done in my life and my relationships with friends and family. Sometimes it's easy to forget that God moves in my life every day or doubt that God is there, but the jar also helps remind me that God loves me. The thankful slips I've written down help me remember he is real and he has moved in my own life!

And when I doubt and can't think of something to be thankful for? I remind myself of the truth from the verse above.

God loves us every day.

And his love endures forever.

Thank you, God.

DEAR GOD,

Thank you for this verse that reminds me that you are good, that you are always loving, and that I should be more thankful. May I remember to thank you so I can trust in you for the times ahead. Will you help me to focus more on the good today than the bad? In Jesus's name I pray,

AMEN.

> *Do not pronounce judgment before the time, before the Lord comes, who will bring to light the things now hidden in darkness and will disclose the purposes of the heart. Then each one will receive his commendation from God.*
>
> **1 CORINTHIANS 4:5** ESV

WESTLEIGH SAYS…

I feel like I'm always trying to do the right thing.

I try to always be kind and make others feel included.

I try to tell the truth.

I try to listen to my teachers and my parents.

And when I'm trying so hard to be good?

I want everyone around me to notice.

It's human nature to want to walk around and think, *Everyone look at me! I'm trying to be good! Aren't you proud?*

When we look to our left and right and see nonbelievers following the ways of this world and misbehaving, sometimes we want to look them up and down and judge them.

We pat ourselves on the back and think we are better. Inside our hearts, we pass judgment on their behavior and tell ourselves, *Thank goodness we aren't like them.*

But are we really better?

No.

We aren't.

We are sinners too.

For example, just because we are choosing actions that aren't wrong doesn't mean that our thoughts are always good. Did you ever think about how rude it might be to think mean and un-Christlike thoughts?

I struggle with this a lot. There are multiple instances when people compliment my actions and I just want to cry because I know I don't deserve them. It makes me feel guilty because I know I'm thinking badly of others who aren't trying to be good.

The light that is shined on our good deeds should be turned around and shined on who Jesus is, not who we are.

That's why Jesus is so amazing.

He looks at our hearts and knows our thoughts and forgives us.

He sees our sin and loves us anyway.

No one is perfect. I love Matthew 7:5, which says, "First take the plank out of your own eye, and then you will see clearly to remove the speck from your brother's eye" (NIV).

How is your heart?

Remind yourself that Jesus knows you aren't perfect.

And he loves you anyway.

DEAR GOD,

Help me to stop worrying about those around me. I need you just as much as they do every day. Humble me, God. Help purify my thoughts and intentions so they are not for selfish ambition or gain but for your glory and yours alone.

AMEN.

You will show me the way of life, granting me the joy of your presence and the pleasures of living with you forever.

PSALM 16:11

WHITNEY SAYS…

D o you ever wonder what the future is going to look like? There are days when I wish I had a time machine so I could see everything that's going to happen in my life.

I want to see who I'll be friends with.

I want to see if I'm going to get married.

I want to see what my job will be when I grow up.

It would make everything so much easier.

Lately I've been trying to decide something, and I've been praying about what I'm supposed to do.

But the answer still isn't clear.

I don't know which way to go and what to decide. This is when a time machine would really come in handy. I could just take a ride into the future to see how my decision turns out.

Have you ever prayed about a decision like me?

Sometimes I wish God would just verbally tell me what he wants me to do or show me what the future looks like.

But here's the thing: If that were the case, then I wouldn't have to depend on God.

I know God wants us to depend on him.

As I've prayed about my decision, I have dwelled on this

verse and recited it over and over. It helps me remember that God will reveal to me what his plans are as I move forward.

I have faith that God will help me work out the answer. I think it's important when you have a big decision to put your focus on God. Don't focus on the problem or worry about the answer. Instead, praise God for what he's already done and lean on faith.

You don't need a time machine.

You have an amazing God to help you instead.

Is there a decision you are having a hard time with?

Have you talked about it with God?

He's here for you.

HI, GOD.

Thank you for this day. Thank you that you are with me in every choice I make, big or small. Thank you that joy is found when you are with me and I am focused on you. Will you help me keep my eyes on you? In your amazing name I pray,

AMEN.

> *You have given me greater joy*
> *than those who have abundant*
> *harvests of grain and new wine.*
>
> **PSALM 4:7**

WHITNEY SAYS…

Do you know the difference between joy and happiness? I know they sound the same, but they are actually really different. Happiness is an emotion we feel for a moment.

It's what you feel when you run downstairs on Christmas morning.

Or score the winning soccer goal.

Or watch your mom fix your favorite dinner.

Maybe you are happy when you're hanging out with your best friend, you get an A on your test, or you are going to the movies on a Saturday? These are all awesome things, but the happiness you receive from these things is only temporary.

That's right.

That dinner probably tastes amazing. Trust me, I love macaroni and cheese. It's my favorite dinner, but that excitement and happiness go away after I eat it.

Why?

This is because all those things I mentioned are earthly things.

Happiness is here for a minute.

But joy?

Joy is what happens when Jesus fills your heart.

Have you heard of something being called a heavenly thing? When we talk about heavenly things, we mean things that please God.

And when we take our focus off ourselves and we are focused on heavenly things and things that please God, our hearts are filled with joy.

Happiness is temporary, but joy is permanent.

My heart is the most excited when I am thinking about the goodness of God or experiencing something good he has done in my life. God wants us to be excited about him. He gives us joy when we are doing things that please him, like loving others or helping our parents or sharing about the things he has done. When we please him, he fills us with joy.

And that joy stays with us.

It doesn't go away after the dinner is finished.

It doesn't go away after Christmas morning is over.

Joy is here to stay, and it's in our hearts.

Have you experienced the joy from God that is greater than everything else?

How can you help others find joy today?

Hi, GOD.

Thank you that true joy is found from doing what you want me to do. Thank you that your love is everlasting and never changes. Will you help me to seek you first before earthly things? In your name I pray,

AMEN.

> *He has shown you, O mortal, what is good. And what does the LORD require of you? To act justly and to love mercy and to walk humbly with your God.*
>
> **MICAH 6:8** NIV

WESTLEIGH SAYS…

What does it mean to love mercy?

Or walk humbly or act justly?

God shows us the perfect example of what it means to do these things.

When Jesus came down to earth, he taught others how to love. People were mean to him, and he turned the other cheek. People let him down, and he still forgave them. Even his disciples messed up, and he showed them grace.

That's just like us—we mess up a lot.

And when we mess up and make choices that aren't the best, we just look to Jesus's example.

Even when we don't feel like it.

He wants us to love mercy and love on everyone, including those who don't love us back.

He wants us to walk humbly with him and tell him of our faults so we can try to live as blamelessly as possible.

I know it's hard sometimes to try to be good, but the sweet thing is that the Lord already knows we're sinners. We don't have to work to earn our place in heaven. We just have to ask him to forgive us and accept what we can give.

So I want to follow Jesus's example every day. Not because I have to, to keep my spot in heaven, but because I want to express my appreciation for the Lord and worship him. I want to give him back anything I can, knowing I can never repay what he's done for me.

Jesus took all our sins upon that cross, even the ones we haven't committed yet.

How can you repay someone for an act like that?

You can't.

But God doesn't want anything but our worship and praise. He just wants to be close to us. Call out to him today and just give him some of your time. Make a point to prioritize him today, and try to practice acting justly, loving mercy, and walking humbly.

What can you do to honor God today?

DEAR GOD,

Help me not to get lost in the act of doing these things to "be good" or work my way to you, but help me remember that I want to show others your love and be like you. Remind me to be like this today.

AMEN.

> *In their hearts humans plan their course,*
> *but the LORD establishes their steps.*
>
> **PROVERBS 16:9** NIV

WHITNEY SAYS…

I don't really like to practice.

I mean, it's okay. But it's a lot of work.

My dance team has been practicing for our dance competition for months and months and months.

There are so many different steps and so much choreography to learn that it takes hours and hours of practice.

And all that practicing is designed to get us ready for the contest ahead.

Our coach wants us to practice so we'll have muscle memory.

Do you know what muscle memory is?

It's when your legs and your arms and your fingers and your toes know what to do automatically, without you even having to tell them.

That's what reading the Bible does for us as Christians.

It's like having our very own "muscle memory."

Except this time—the muscle is our brain.

We face a lot of challenging things in our lives. We don't do well on tests, or we get into arguments with our best friends, or we think our parents aren't listening to us.

Instead of overreacting and saying things we don't mean or making choices that aren't the best, we should use Scripture to guide us.

When faced with a challenge or a situation that is a little overwhelming, we should rely on what the Bible tells us.

Reading Scriptures and memorizing them helps us with our "muscle memory." I am so happy I was in Bible Drill when we were younger because it gave us such a great foundation to build on. I still try to read and memorize Scriptures now by writing them on Post-it notes and sticking them around my room.

It helps me so much to know that we can have God's Word to rely on without even thinking about it or worrying we don't know what to do. When I leave my room to face the world, it helps to have God's truth in my head as a reminder of how to live for God.

God has the perfect plan for our lives.

We just have to remember to rely on his Word and what he shows us is best for us.

Are you memorizing Scripture?

How is your muscle memory?

Hi, GOD.

Thank you for loving me like you do. Thank you for giving me the Bible to read and helping me with my muscle memory. Thank you for caring about me enough to show me your Word. In your awesome name I pray,

AMEN.

> *Let everything that has breath*
> *praise the L*ORD*. Praise the L*ORD*.*
>
> **PSALM 150:6** NIV

WESTLEIGH SAYS…

Remember when God created the universe?

He created Adam and Eve and all the creatures big and small.

And when he finished, he was glad and happy with what he created.

Sometimes we forget that the Lord created all the beautiful things of the earth. We should be praising his name all the time.

When you look back at your life, isn't it cool that things intertwine so well?

It's easy to say, "Well that's a coincidence!"

But if you think about it—is it a coincidence?

Or is it God?

Like when you don't want to go to the grocery store with your mom, but you go anyway. And then? There at the store, you end up talking to a sweet lady about her daughter.

Maybe God needed you on that grocery run just so you could have the opportunity to share Jesus with her.

I want to encourage you to stop and take a moment to think today about all the little "coincidences" like that in your life.

Is there a reason your spring break plans didn't go as you intended?

Did God allow you to spend family time at home bonding? Or help out a neighbor?

So many times, you don't understand why things happened the way they did until you look back.

Hindsight shows you how God was there all along, making plans.

I get overwhelmed when I think about the goodness of God and his ultimate plan for my life.

He created the heavens and the earth and the skies and the seas and the creatures here—from the tiniest insect to the largest whale.

And we are part of that plan too.

It's important to remember why we were created on this earth.

We are here to bring glory to his name and share his love with others.

All those coincidences are just his way of letting us know he hasn't forgotten about us.

We are part of his creation.

What coincidences can you think of today that worked as part of God's plan?

GOD,

Help reveal your goodness to me today. Help me to remember all the times in my life that you have intersected to help me and to bring people to come to know you. Lord, help me to praise your name above any other name or thing of this world. You are so, so good. In your name,

AMEN.

> *I lift up my eyes to the mountains—*
> *where does my help come from?*
> *My help comes from the Lord, the*
> *Maker of heaven and earth.*
>
> **PSALM 121:1-2** NIV

WHITNEY SAYS...

I smile whenever I see a sunset.

When was the last time you looked at the sky? Were there lots of colors?

The layers and the brilliance and the way the light spreads out across the sky during a sunset is amazing.

Sometimes I run when the sun is setting just so I can see the sunset at the top of a hill in my neighborhood.

Sunsets and beautiful things in nature remind me of God.

Like the flowers that bloom in our yard in the spring.

And the trees with their branches that shade the yard.

And the blue sky on a summer day.

God created all these amazing things just for us.

All the beauty in nature reminds me there is a world around that is so much bigger than me.

It helps me put everything into perspective and reminds me that I shouldn't be discouraged by small situations that frustrate me—like feeling left out or getting a bad grade on a test. It's so easy to be stubborn and think the little things we are upset about are so much more important than they actually are.

Sometimes we just need to change our attitude and not let the little things get us down.

When I get frustrated with small situations, I try to take a walk and spend time with Jesus. It makes my heart so happy to get outside and see all the beautiful things around me.

When we let little things get us down, it's a great reminder that we aren't perfect.

And the best part?

We don't have to be.

We have a perfect God who is there for us.

A God who loves us so much that he created a beautiful world for us to live in with flowers and clouds and blue skies.

And sunsets.

Take a moment today to look at the world around you.

Have you thanked God for it lately?

Hi, God.

Thank you for your beautiful creation. Thank you for beautiful sunsets that portray you. Thank you that in the same way, you made me carefully and beautifully. Will you help me to try to meet with you more so I can be reminded to be calm? In your awesome name I pray,

AMEN.

Westleigh Wood is older than her sister by one minute and has never met a glitter glue project she didn't like. She's been creating and drawing and Pinteresting since her first unsolicited black marker wall in preschool.

Whitney Wood is all about sticky notes. She covered an entire wall (and a few other ancillary accessories) with Bible verses and inspirational quotes written on hundreds of colorful sticky notes squares. She draws, paints, builds, and creates one-of-a-kind flower crowns for her friends.

KariAnne Wood writes the award-winning lifestyle blog *Thistlewood Farms*, a tiny corner of the internet where all her stories and DIY's hang out and drink sweet tea. She also writes, photographs, and styles for several national magazines, including *Better Homes and Gardens Christmas Ideas*, *Country Women*, and *Flea Market Décor*.

BUILD YOUR CONFIDENCE AND CREATIVITY

Cell phones and tablets are fun, but they can't replace the simple joy of making something of your very own. With these 52 DIY activities—a new project for every week of the year—you'll discover you can accomplish anything you set your mind to.

Each craft is illustrated and includes easy-to-understand instructions. In addition, each DIY shows the supplies you'll need, how easy or difficult it is, how much it will cost, and how much time it will take to complete.

Nothing hard. Nothing complicated. Just easy and fun projects for you to enjoy by yourself or with friends or family!

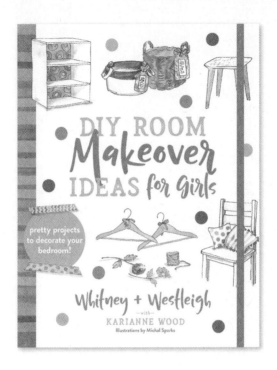

YOUR ROOM IS SPECIAL...JUST LIKE YOU!

Your bedroom is one of the few places in the world you can truly call your own. Now you can decorate your space to make your room reflect your unique personality.

Whitney and Westleigh offer you a year's worth of pretty projects that will transform your room to fit your one-of-a-kind style. They include fun and colorful crafts for your windows, walls, door, and so much more!

Each craft has illustrated and easy-to-follow instructions. You'll also see the supplies you'll need, how easy or difficult it is, how much it will cost, and how much time it will take to complete.

As you begin creating, drawing, and painting, you'll see your creativity and confidence grow!

To learn more about Harvest House books and
to read sample chapters, visit our website:

www.harvesthousepublishers.com

HARVEST HOUSE PUBLISHERS
EUGENE, OREGON